100
YEARS OF
CRICKET

100
YEARS OF
CRICKET

PA Photos

AMMONITE
PRESS

First published 2008 by

AMMONITE PRESS

an imprint of AE Publications Ltd.

166 High Street, Lewes, East Sussex BN7 1XU

ISBN 978-1-906672-00-3

British Cataloguing in Publication Data. A catalogue record of this book is available from the British Library.

Editor **NEIL DUNNICLIFFE**
Designer **JO PATTERSON**

Colour origination by GMC Reprographics
Printed and bound by Colorprint Offset in China

Contents

Chapter One
PEOPLE

THE GREAT AND GOOD

Cricket has always been played by great characters, though they may not always have been famous

Two hundred years ago cricket was a rustic game, played by land owners, farm folk and gardeners to settle rivalries between villages and small towns. Today it is a global industry, watched by millions on television, as countries battle for the Ashes and the World Cup.

Who brought about this slow but significant change? The players certainly played their part, beginning with John Nyren the player and historian of the 18th century, through to the likes of Kevin Pietersen, Michael Vaughan and Andrew Flintoff in the 21st century.

THE PRINCE OF WALES WITH W.G. GRACE. 1911

W.G. GRACE

The first world figure was W.G. Grace. Tall, thin in his youth and thick-set in later life, he found time to make 124 centuries, play all around England in charity matches and by the time his career came to an end he dominated the game everywhere.

Asked to name his world XI, he showed his own certainty that he would be the leading light, as he added: 'Give me Arthur.' He meant Arthur Shrewsbury of Nottinghamshire, a professional in one of the cities where cricket had taken decisive steps forward in the 19th century and later a Test venue.

EARLY 20TH CENTURY

Grace was succeeded by Jack Hobbs, a lad who learnt to play the game in Cambridge, where his father was groundsman. Hobbs still has more centuries to his credit than any other

1940s AND 1950s

England had two batsmen who missed the best years of their careers in World War II – Len Hutton and Denis Compton – but the two blossomed afterwards and Hutton, the first professional captain in the 20th century, regained the Ashes in 1953 after 19 years.

SIXTIES ONWARDS

Hutton's appointment as captain was just one step in the abolition of the line between amateur and professional. There was also a greater emphasis on one-day cricket which became an international fixture in 1971 and grew into the World Cup by 1975.

Soon afterwards West Indies, whose all-rounder Garry Sobers had established the world batting mark, (held by Hutton since 1938) with 365, had become a world force.

batsman. It took him until he was over 50 to make 199 hundreds and it will be a remarkable batsman who will overtake that record.

By this time the game had begun to be dominated by batsmen, as the rough old pitches of the 19th century gave way to close shorn, heavily-rolled strips of what used to be called 'featherbeds' meant to last no more than five days.

BETWEEN THE WARS

Don Bradman and Wally Hammond, perhaps Bradman's closest rival as a run-scoring machine, took advantage in the years between the wars, while bowlers toiled. Except, that is, for the England tour of Australia in 1932-33 when the captain Douglas Jardine launched the speed trio of Harold Larwood, Bill Voce and Bill Bowes and a volley of bouncers.

This was known as 'bodyline' and was designed to stop Bradman in his tracks; instead it almost brought Tests between England and Australia to an end.

ENGLAND CAPTAIN LEN HUTTON (SIXTH L) LEADS THE TEAM ONTO THE FIELD AT LORD'S. 19/06/1952

By the middle of the 1980s their fearsome foursome of fast men had made them world leaders. Viv Richards, with support from Des Haynes and Gordon Greenidge piled up huge scores, and their captain Clive Lloyd ensured that there was a unity within the side.

IAN BOTHAM

England had one player who dominated headlines wherever the game was played.

Ian Botham was a great character who broke records and won Tests. He also walked thousands of miles to raise millions of pounds for charity and 25 years on, received a knighthood.

Briefly he, Graham Gooch and David Gower ensured England kept the Ashes. Botham retired with 383 wickets and 5200 runs.

THE 1990s

In the 1990s the Australians, now coached by their former captain Bobby Simpson and led by Alan Border, became a feared and formidable team. When Simpson stepped down, John Buchanan took them forward with continued success.

The retirement of Shane Warne with 708 Test wickets – since overtaken by Muttiah Muralitharan, like Warne a spin bowler – and Glenn McGrath, with 500 wickets seems to have made no difference.

England won the Ashes in 2005 but 18 months later Australia won the tiny urn back with a devastating 5-0 whitewash.

Powerful batsmen like Vaughan, Pietersen, Andrew Strauss, Ian Bell, and Paul Collingwood as well as a pace attack consisting of Flintoff, Steve Harmison, Matthew Hoggard and James Anderson have made England a formidable side.

THE FUTURE

Now the world awaits the next great cricketer. Will he come from Australia where their success is the national obsession as well as the country's favourite game? From West Indies, where the passion for cricket is undiminished? Or South Africa?

Perhaps the next great star will be an England player. Pietersen, a real force, Vaughan, a wonderful technician, and

IAN BOTHAM, SOMERSET.
02/09/1978

Flintoff, everyone's favourite fast bowler and quick scorer, offer the obvious choices.

All descend from those farm lads in the 18th century, not one of them dreaming that their humble pastime would one day be the talk of the world.

ENGLAND'S ANDREW FLINTOFF.
12/08/2004

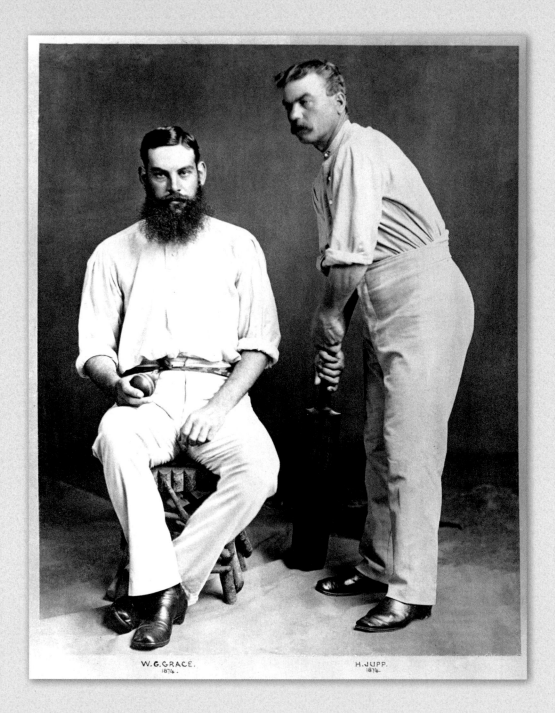

W.G.GRACE.
1874.

H.JUPP.
1874.

OPPOSITE

W.G. GRACE (L), GLOUCESTERSHIRE
AND ENGLAND, AND HARRY JUPP (R),
SURREY AND ENGLAND. 1874

LUDFORD DOCKER, WARWICKSHIRE.
1895

JOHN HILL, WARWICKSHIRE. 1895

OPPOSITE

SCHOFIELD HAIGH, YORKSHIRE. 1900

WILFRED RHODES, ENGLAND. 1902

THE ENGLAND TEAM THAT TOURED AUSTRALIA: (BACK ROW, L-R) DICK LILLEY, ALBERT KNIGHT, ARTHUR FIELDER, TED ARNOLD, ALBERT RELF, LEN BRAUND; (MIDDLE ROW, L-R) JOHNNY TYLDESLEY, TIP FOSTER, PELHAM 'PLUM' WARNER, GEORGE HIRST, BERNARD BOSANQUET, TOM HAYWARD; (FRONT ROW, L-R) BERT STRUDWICK, WILFRED RHODES. 1903

W.G. GRACE. HE PLAYED IN THE FIRST TEST MATCH IN ENGLAND – AGAINST AUSTRALIA IN 1880 AT THE OVAL – AND SCORED THE FIRST TEST CENTURY BY AN ENGLISH BATSMAN. 1905

OPPOSITE

C.B. FRY ON CRUTCHES AFTER INJURING ONE OF HIS ANKLES. 1908

PATSY HENDREN, MIDDLESEX
AND ENGLAND. 1924

COL. J.T.C. MOORE-BRABAZON, MP, GOING OUT TO BAT IN THE FIRST PARLIAMENTARY CRICKET MATCH AT THE OVAL.
08/05/1924

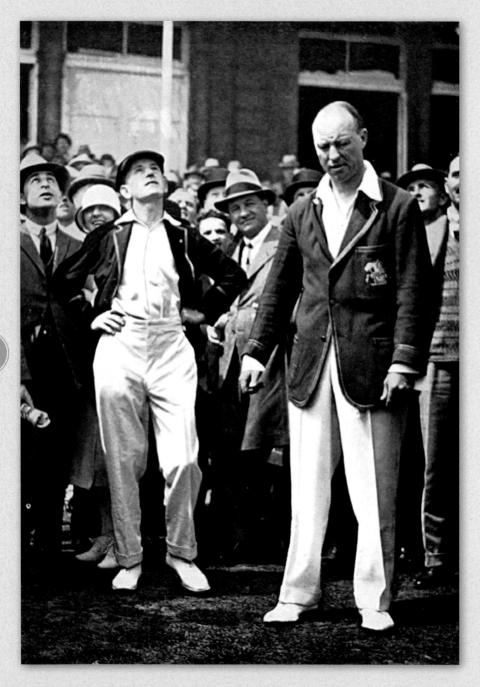

AUSTRALIA CAPTAIN HERBIE COLLINS
(L) AND ENGLAND CAPTAIN ARTHUR
CARR (R), AT THE COIN TOSS.
26/06/1926

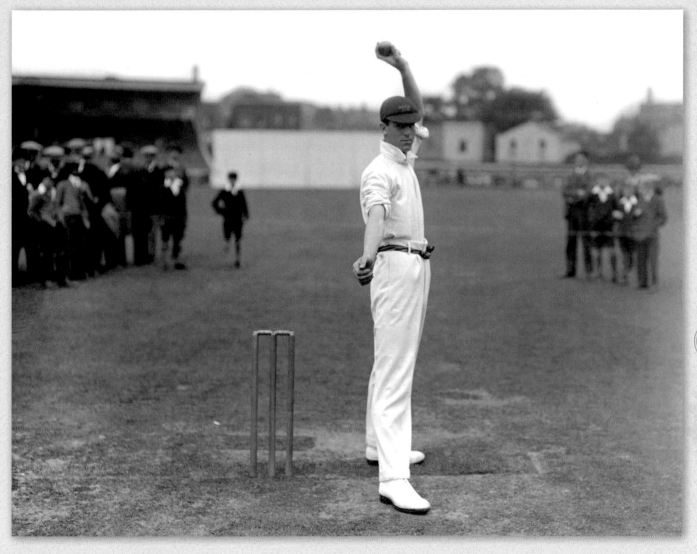

BILL VOCE, NOTTINGHAMSHIRE. 02/08/1927

SOUTH AFRICA'S TUPPY OWEN-SMITH
(R) BATTING IN FRONT OF
WICKETKEEPER JOCK CAMERON (L)
AT NETS DURING A TOUR OF
ENGLAND. 27/04/1929

AUSTRALIA'S DON BRADMAN AND
STAN MCCABE MAKE THEIR WAY TO
THE WICKET AGAINST ENGLAND AT
HEADINGLEY. 14/07/1930

HAROLD LARWOOD (L) AND BILL VOCE (R), NOTTINGHAMSHIRE. 02/08/1932

ENGLAND CAPTAIN DOUGLAS
JARDINE (R) AND TEAMMATE PELHAM
'PLUM' WARNER (L) LOOK PLEASED
TO HAVE FINALLY ARRIVED IN
AUSTRALIA. 15/11/1932

AUSTRALIA CAPTAIN, BILL WOODFULL (L) AND ENGLAND CAPTAIN, DOUGLAS JARDINE (R), AT THE COIN TOSS. 23/02/1933

MARJORIE POLLARD, ENGLAND
CRICKET AND HOCKEY CAPTAIN.
22/05/1934

MAURICE TURNBULL, GLAMORGAN.
01/05/1937

OPPOSITE

AUSTRALIA'S BILL O'REILLY (R) TAKES
A SWING AT A NO-BALL AND IS CLEAN
BOWLED, WATCHED BY ENGLAND
WICKETKEEPER LES AMES (L).
27/06/1938

AUSTRALIA CAPTAIN LINDSAY
HASSETT (R) TALKS TO ENGLAND
CAPTAIN WALLY HAMMOND (L)
BEFORE THE START OF PLAY AT
LORD'S. 14/07/1945

INDIA'S OPENING BATSMEN MUSHTAQ ALI (L) AND VIJAY MERCHANT (R) MAKE
THEIR WAY TO THE CREASE AGAINST ENGLAND AT OLD TRAFFORD. 22/07/1946

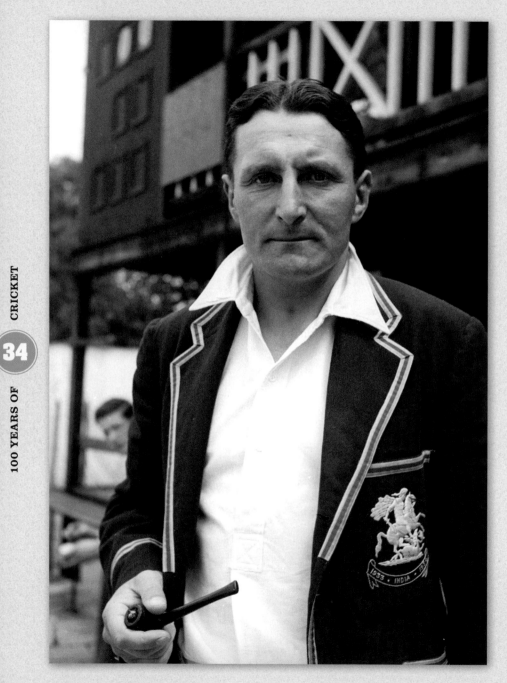

CHARLIE BARNETT,
GLOUCESTERSHIRE. 01/07/1947

OPPOSITE

THE BEDSER TWINS OF SURREY, ERIC
(L) AND ALEC (R). 12/07/1947

HUBERT DOGGART, CAMBRIDGE
UNIVERSITY. 12/05/1948

OPPOSITE

LEN HUTTON, THE YORKSHIRE PLAYER, WAVES FAREWELL FROM THE BOAT-TRAIN AT WATERLOO STATION. 07/10/1948

SURREY AND ENGLAND'S JACK HOBBS DISPLAYS HIS BATTING TECHNIQUE TO YOUNGSTERS IN THE NETS. 01/08/1949

OPPOSITE

WARWICKSHIRE'S ALAN TOWNSEND
(L) CLIPS THE BALL OFF HIS PADS,
WATCHED BY ESSEX WICKETKEEPER
TOM WADE (R). 03/06/1950

YORKSHIRE'S LEN HUTTON (L) AND
FRANK LOWSON (R) WALK OUT TO
OPEN THE BATTING. 22/06/1950

PEOPLE

41

CHAPTER ONE

ENGLAND'S TREVOR BAILEY
(BOTTOM) APPEALS FOR LBW
AGAINST AUSTRALIA'S KEITH MILLER
(TOP). 26/12/1950

ENGLAND CAPTAIN FREDDIE BROWN
CELEBRATES VICTORY IN THE FINAL
ASHES TEST. 28/02/1951

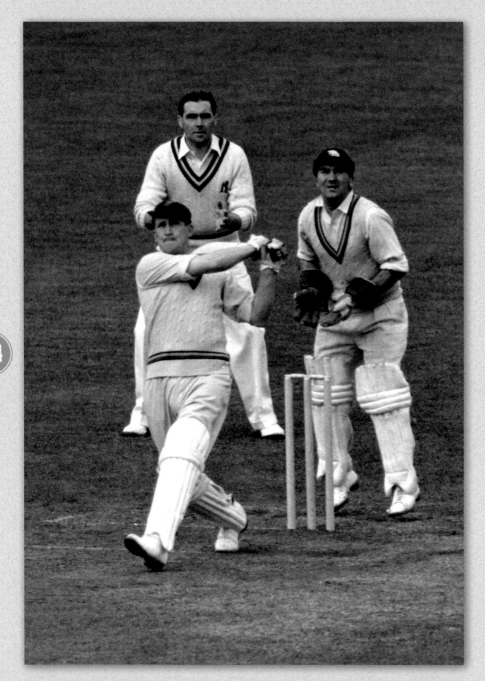

SURREY'S JIM LAKER (L) SLOGS
A BOUNDARY, WATCHED BY MCC
WICKETKEEPER GODFREY EVANS (R).
08/05/1953

ALAN DAVIDSON OF AUSTRALIA
BOWLING IN THE NETS DURING
A TOUR OF ENGLAND. 24/06/1953

OPPOSITE

SUSSEX'S KEN SUTTLE RUNS ALONG
THE BEACH AT WORTHING TO KEEP
HIS FITNESS HIGH FOR THE
FORTHCOMING MCC TOUR OF THE
WEST INDIES. 30/11/1953

DENIS COMPTON (C) PUSHES THE
BALL THROUGH THE SLIPS. 14/07/1954

DES BARRICK (L) AND FRANK TYSON
(R), NORTHAMPTONSHIRE. 21/07/1954

OPPOSITE

GLAMORGAN'S WILF WOOLLER (L)
HITS OUT, WATCHED BY MIDDLESEX
WICKETKEEPER LES COMPTON (C).
23/07/1954

AUSTRALIA'S RICHIE BENAUD
(SECOND L) TAKES EVASIVE ACTION
AS ENGLAND'S TREVOR BAILEY (R)
ATTEMPTS TO SWEEP A BALL FROM
IAN JOHNSON (THIRD R). 01/12/1954

CAPTAIN LEN HUTTON SHOWING
HIS PLEASURE AFTER ENGLAND'S FIVE
WICKET WIN OVER AUSTRALIA IN THE
FOURTH TEST MATCH AT ADELAIDE
OVAL. 07/02/1955

TREVOR BAILEY DEMONSTRATES A
STROKE FOR YOUNGER MEMBERS OF
THE ESSEX COUNTY CRICKET CLUB.
20/04/1956

OPPOSITE

ENGLAND'S FRED TRUEMAN (R)
CHATS WITH AUSTRALIA'S RAY
LINDWALL (L) AHEAD OF THE ASHES
SERIES. 27/04/1956

WORCESTERSHIRE COUNTY CRICKET
CLUB TEAM GROUP. 1956

OPPOSITE

BRIAN STATHAM BOWLING. 1956

ENGLAND'S JIM LAKER TOASTS
VICTORY WITH A GLASS OF
CHAMPAGNE AFTER TAKING SIX
SECOND INNINGS WICKETS AGAINST
AUSTRALIA. 17/07/1956

OPPOSITE

THE ENGLAND TEAM BOARD THE
EDINBURGH CASTLE BOAT/TRAIN
FOR SOUTH AFRICA. SURREY AND
ENGLAND'S TONY LOCK KISSES HIS
3 YEAR OLD SON GRAEME GOODBYE
AS HIS WIFE AUDREY LOOKS ON.
04/10/1956

WESTERN PROVINCE'S TONY PITHEY
(C) PULLS ENGLAND'S PETER LOADER
(R) TO BACKWARD SQUARE LEG.
28/10/1956

OPPOSITE

THE FAST BOWLER ROY GILCHRIST (L) AND THE YOUNGEST MEMBER OF THE
PARTY, 19 YEAR OLD WES HALL, DISCUSS THE FORTHCOMING TOUR OF
ENGLAND TOGETHER AS THEY ARRIVE IN SOUTHAMPTON WITH THE WEST
INDIES TEAM. 14/04/1957

PASSENGERS NOT
ALLOWED BEYOND
THESE RAILS

THE ENGLAND WOMEN'S CRICKET
TEAM. 29/07/1957

OPPOSITE

GAMINI GOONESENA, EW
SWANTON'S XI AND CAMBRIDGE
UNIVERSITY. 29/04/1957

ROY SWETMAN, SURREY. 1958

OPPOSITE

NAREN TAMHANE, INDIA, DURING A
TOUR OF ENGLAND. 21/04/1959

MCC'S FRANK TYSON (C) BOWLING.

05/05/1959

OPPOSITE

PETER MARNER (LANCASHIRE) CUTS
THE BALL TO MIDDLESEX FIELDER
FRED TITMUS. 23/07/1959

WEST INDIES' GARRY SOBERS (L)
TAKES A SINGLE OFF THE LAST BALL
OF THE DAY TO COMPLETE HIS
CENTURY AGAINST ENGLAND.
09/01/1960

OPPOSITE

RICHIE BENAUD, AUSTRALIA CAPTAIN,
IN THE NETS AT LORD'S. 27/04/1961

ENGLAND'S FRED TRUEMAN TOASTS
VICTORY AFTER COMPILING MATCH
FIGURES OF 11 WICKETS FOR 88 RUNS
AGAINST AUSTRALIA AT HEADINGLEY.
08/07/1961

OPPOSITE

HANIF MOHAMMAD, PAKISTAN, IN
THE NETS AT LORD'S. 26/04/1962

OPPOSITE

ENGLAND'S TOM GRAVENEY WALKS BACK TO THE
PAVILION AFTER BEING DISMISSED FOR 153, THE LAST
MAN OUT IN ENGLAND'S FIRST INNINGS AGAINST
PAKISTAN. 22/06/1962

SOUTH AUSTRALIA'S IAN CHAPPELL (ON FLOOR) BREAKS
HIS OWN WICKET AFTER A SWINGING DELIVERY FROM
ENGLAND'S BRIAN STATHAM (TOP R). 02/11/1962

SOUTH AUSTRALIA'S GARRY SOBERS
(R) NARROWLY ESCAPES DISMISSAL AS
MCC WICKETKEEPER ALAN SMITH
(TOP, C) APPEALS. 06/11/1962

MCC'S COLIN COWDREY (L) AND
TOM GRAVENEY (R). 24/12/1962

OPPOSITE

WES HALL, THE WEST INDIES
FAST BOWLER, FALLS AS BRIAN CLOSE
(L) AND FRED TITMUS OF ENGLAND
SCRAMBLE FOR A QUICK SINGLE.
25/06/1963

ENGLAND'S MICKY STEWART DIVES
TO TAKE A CATCH. 22/06/1963

KEN BARRINGTON, SURREY AND
ENGLAND. 01/07/1963

OPPOSITE
(L-R) RICHARD HUTTON (CAMBRIDGE) TALKS WITH HIS FATHER SIR LEN HUTTON
AND THE NAWAB OF PATAUDI (OXFORD). 13/07/1963

YORKSHIRE'S SCORER ED LESTER
MAKES HIS WAY OUT ONTO THE
FIELD. 27/05/1964

FRED TRUEMAN OFFERS UP A PRAYER BEFORE FACING HIS FIRST BALL FROM
WES HALL (NOT IN PIC), TO THE AMUSEMENT OF WICKETKEEPER JOHN MURRAY.
30/07/1964

GEOFF BOYCOTT, YORKSHIRE AND
ENGLAND. 22/06/1965

MIDDLESEX WICKETKEEPER JOHN
MURRAY WITH A MAN OF THE MATCH
AWARD. 23/06/1965

YORKSHIRE'S BRIAN CLOSE HOOKS
THE BALL TO THE BOUNDARY.
04/09/1965

OPPOSITE

WEST INDIES STAR LANCE GIBBS
CATCHES UP ON THE NEWS AS HE
WAITS FOR HIS TURN TO BAT FOR THE
REST OF THE WORLD SIDE AGAINST
ENGLAND. 08/09/1965

BRIAN CLOSE AT HOME. 28/09/1965

OPPOSITE

ENGLAND'S GEOFF BOYCOTT (L) AND
COLIN MILBURN (R) WALK OUT TO
OPEN THE BATTING. 17/06/1966

(L-R) HANIF, MUSHTAQ AND SADIQ MOHAMMAD OF PAKISTAN DURING A TOUR

OF ENGLAND. 20/06/1967

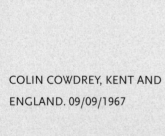

COLIN COWDREY, KENT AND
ENGLAND. 09/09/1967

OPPOSITE

IAN CHAPPELL, AUSTRALIA. 01/05/1968

VICTORIOUS YORKSHIRE SKIPPER
FREDDIE TRUEMAN TAKES A WELL-
EARNED DRINK AFTER YORKSHIRE'S
VICTORY OVER AUSTRALIA AT
BRAMALL LANE, SHEFFIELD.
02/07/1968

OPPOSITE

GORDON BARKER OF ESSEX AT
BATTING PRACTICE IN CHELMSFORD.
24/04/1969

JOHN LEVER OF ESSEX AT BOWLING
PRACTICE IN CHELMSFORD.
24/04/1969

OPPOSITE
MIKE BREARLEY, MIDDLESEX.
27/04/1969

OPPOSITE

REST OF THE WORLD'S GRAEME
POLLOCK PADS UP FOR NETS DURING
A TOUR OF ENGLAND. 15/06/1970

ENGLAND CAPTAIN RAY
ILLINGWORTH (L) AND REST OF THE
WORLD XI CAPTAIN GARRY SOBERS (R)
AFTER THE TOSS-UP. 17/06/1970

MCC'S GEOFF BOYCOTT (L) AND
JOHN JAMESON (R) WALK OUT TO
OPEN THE BATTING. 22/05/1972

AUSTRALIA CAPTAIN IAN CHAPPELL (L)
LOOKS ON AS ENGLAND CAPTAIN RAY
ILLINGWORTH (R) CHECKS THE
WEATHER CONDITIONS. 22/06/1972

ENGLAND'S DEREK UNDERWOOD
RELAXES AS HE STUDIES PICTURES OF
SOME OF HIS 10 WICKETS FROM THE
MATCH. THIRD DAY OF THE FOURTH
ASHES TEST. 29/07/1972

OPPOSITE

ENGLAND OPENER GEOFF BOYCOTT
WITH A TRAY OF DRINKS AND
MAURICE FOSTER OF THE WEST
INDIES, CARRYING TOWELS, DURING
A BREAK IN PLAY ON THE FOURTH
DAY OF THE SECOND TEST BETWEEN
ENGLAND AND THE WEST INDIES AT
EDGBASTON. 13/08/1973

ENGLAND'S CHRIS OLD TAKES A
BREAK TO CHANGE HIS BAT AFTER
THE HANDLE SNAPPED. 09/08/1974

SUSSEX CAPTAIN TONY GREIG
EXAMINES A WAXWORK OF HIMSELF,
MADE FOR INCLUSION IN A MADAME
TUSSAUD'S EXHIBITION. 15/09/1975

OPPOSITE

WEST INDIES' VIV RICHARDS TAKES A
BREATHER WITH BATTING PARTNER
ALVIN KALLICHARRAN (R) DURING
THE OPENING DAY'S PLAY OF THE
FIRST TEST MATCH AGAINST
ENGLAND. 03/06/1976

BRIAN CLOSE MAKES A DIVING ATTEMPT AT A CHANCE OFFERED BY ROY
FREDERICKS OF THE WEST INDIES OFF THE BOWLING OF MIKE HENDRICK (ARMS
RAISED). 09/07/1976

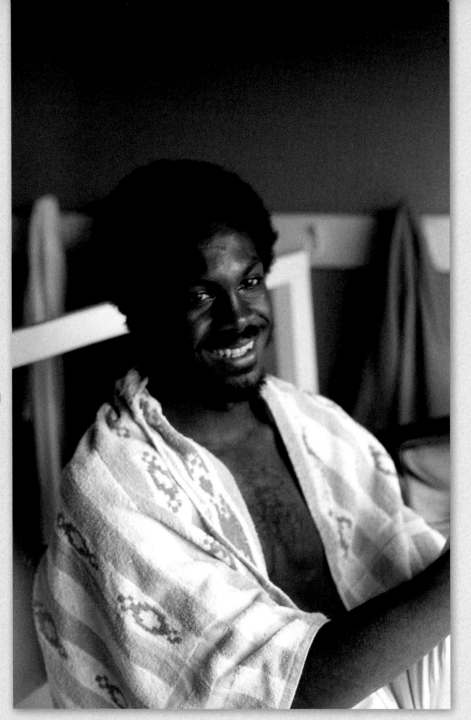

WEST INDIES' MICHAEL HOLDING, CELEBRATING WINNING THE TEST SERIES AGAINST ENGLAND AT THE OVAL. 17/08/1976

OPPOSITE

IAN BOTHAM, ENGLAND. 12/08/1977

ENGLAND AND MIDDLESEX CAPTAIN
MIKE BREARLEY (R) WITH IAN
BOTHAM OF SOMERSET (L) AND PAUL
DOWNTON OF KENT, AFTER THE
LATTER PAIR HAD EACH RECEIVED
AWARDS AT THE LORD'S TAVERNERS
BMW CRICKET AWARDS FOR FIRST
CLASS CRICKETERS UNDER THE AGE
OF 25. BOTHAM PICKED UP TWO
AWARDS AS BEST ALL-ROUNDER AND
BEST FIELDER AND DOWNTON WAS
NAMED AS BEST WICKETKEEPER. IN
ADDITION, BREARLEY WON THE
CRICKETER OF THE YEAR AWARD.
23/11/1977

ENGLAND'S GEOFF BOYCOTT WIPES
THE SWEAT FROM HIS BROW.
23/06/1979

UMPIRE BARRIE MEYER (L) SHARES A JOKE WITH ENGLAND CAPTAIN MIKE BREARLEY (R). 12/07/1979

THE POWELL TWIN SISTERS, JILL (L) AND JANE, GETTING READY AT LORD'S TO PLAY FOR YOUNG ENGLAND AGAINST THE WEST INDIES TOURING TEAM IN THE LIMITED-OVER MATCH AT THE OVAL. 01/08/1979

OPPOSITE

ENGLAND'S IAN BOTHAM RACES
BACK TO THE EDGBASTON PAVILION
WITH A SOUVENIR STUMP IN HIS
HAND AFTER ENGLAND WON THE
FOURTH TEST AGAINST AUSTRALIA.
02/08/1981

ENGLAND CAPTAIN KEITH FLETCHER
WAVES GOODBYE AS HE PREPARES TO
DEPART FOR INDIA. 04/11/1981

ENGLAND CAPTAIN BOB WILLIS
SITTING OUT THE SECOND TEST
AGAINST PAKISTAN AT LORD'S.
12/08/1982

YORKSHIRE'S RAY ILLINGWORTH (R)
TAKES EVASIVE ACTION AS
MIDDLESEX'S ROLAND BUTCHER (L)
DRIVES A BALL TO THE BOUNDARY.
23/08/1982

MIDDLESEX'S CLIVE RADLEY (R) LEAPS
OUT OF THE WAY AS SOMERSET'S VIV
RICHARDS (L) CUTS THE BALL
SQUARE. 20/08/1983

OPPOSITE

FRED TRUEMAN, OLD ENGLAND XI.
17/09/1983

ENGLAND'S IAN BOTHAM (L)
CONGRATULATES TEAMMATE
GRAHAM FOWLER (R) ON REACHING
HIS CENTURY AGAINST WEST INDIES.
29/06/1984

OPPOSITE

FIVE COMPETITORS IN THE SILK CUT CHALLENGE – A TOURNAMENT DESIGNED
TO FIND THE WORLD'S TOP ALL-ROUNDER. FROM FRONT: RICHARD HADLEE,
CLIVE RICE, KAPIL DEV, IAN BOTHAM AND MALCOLM MARSHALL. 15/09/1984

AUSTRALIA'S ALLAN BORDER
(BOTTOM) DUCKS UNDER A BOUNCER
FROM ENGLAND'S IAN BOTHAM
(TOP). 29/06/1985

LEICESTERSHIRE'S LES TAYLOR
CELEBRATES HIS CALL-UP TO THE
ENGLAND SQUAD. 11/08/1985

ENGLAND'S JOHN EMBUREY (L), MIKE GATTING (SECOND L), PAUL DOWNTON
(FIFTH L), PHIL EDMONDS (FOURTH R), DAVID GOWER (THIRD R), IAN BOTHAM
(SECOND R) AND ALLAN LAMB (R) APPEAL FOR THE WICKET OF AUSTRALIA'S
WAYNE PHILLIPS (FOURTH L) FOLLOWING GOWER'S CATCH OF A BALL WHICH
DEFLECTED OFF LAMB'S BOOT. 20/08/1985

OPPOSITE

MIKE GATTING WITH A STITCHED-UP
NOSE AT HEATHROW AIRPORT WHEN
HE ARRIVED BACK FROM THE WEST
INDIES. 23/02/1986

UMPIRE HAROLD 'DICKIE' BIRD GRABS
HIS LEG IN AGONY AFTER BEING HIT
ON THE SHIN BY THE BALL.
08/06/1987

IMRAN KHAN, PAKISTAN,
AT THE OVAL. 10/08/1987

MCC'S GRAHAM GOOCH (L) HITS
OUT, WATCHED BY REST OF THE
WORLD XI WICKETKEEPER JEFF DUJON
(C). 20/08/1987

OPPOSITE

JONATHAN AGNEW, LEICESTERSHIRE.
19/05/1988

FORMER ENGLAND BATSMAN SIR LEN HUTTON RETURNS TO THE CREASE AT THE OVAL WHERE HE SET HIS WORLD RECORD TEST SCORE OF 364 AGAINST AUSTRALIA IN 1938, THE SCOREBOARD IN THE BACKGROUND SHOWING THE MATCH FIGURES AT THE CONCLUSION OF HIS RECORD-BREAKING INNINGS. 23/08/1988

NEW ZEALAND'S RICHARD HADLEE
WATCHES THE MATCH AGAINST
ENGLAND FROM THE OTHER SIDE OF
THE BOUNDARY ROPE AFTER
RETIRING HURT. 25/05/1990

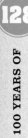

ENGLAND'S GRAHAM GOOCH ON HIS
WAY TO HIS 100TH CENTURY.
23/01/1993

OPPOSITE

DURHAM'S SIMON HUGHES TAKES A
PHOTO OF HIS COLLEAGUE, IAN
BOTHAM. 17/04/1992

BRIAN LARA (WEST INDIES) KISSES THE WICKET THAT GAVE HIM HIS RECORD BREAKING TEST INNINGS AGAINST ENGLAND.
18/04/1994

ENGLAND'S GRAHAM THORPE (R) PLAYS A SWEEP SHOT. 24/08/1995

ENGLAND COACH, DAVID LLOYD
TRIES TO MAKE HIMSELF HEARD AT
NETS. 21/05/1997

OPPOSITE

ADAM HOLLIOAKE, ENGLAND.
13/12/1997

ENGLAND'S ANGUS FRASER DROPS
HIS CATCH ON THE FIRST BALL OF
THE DAY FROM WEST INDIES
BATSMAN DAVID WILLIAMS.
09/02/1998

OPPOSITE

ALEC STEWART, ENGLAND. 20/06/1998

OPPOSITE

ENGLAND'S DARREN GOUGH SHOWS
HIS DISAPPOINTMENT AFTER HIS LBW
APPEAL AGAINST SOUTH AFRICA'S
HANSIE CRONJE WAS TURNED DOWN.
25/07/1998

ENGLAND'S DOMINIC CORK APPEALS.
09/08/1998

ENGLAND'S DARREN GOUGH KICKS
THE BALL IN AN ATTEMPT TO RUN
OUT SOUTH AFRICA'S LANCE
KLUSENER. 22/05/1999

OPPOSITE

DURING THE FIRST DAY OF THE LAST WEEK OF HIS UMPIRING CAREER, 'DICKIE'
BIRD RELAXES WITH A CUP OF TEA IN THE UMPIRES' ROOM AT HEADINGLEY. THE
START OF THE GAME WAS DELAYED BY RAIN. 09/09/1998

LANCASHIRE'S SPIN BOWLER
MUTTIAH MURALITHARAN KEEPS HIS
EYES ON THE BALL AS HE UNLEASHES
A DELIVERY. 15/07/1999

OPPOSITE
GLOUCESTERSHIRE'S ROBERT
CUNLIFFE DIVES TO HIS CREASE.
10/06/2000

CRICKET

140

100 YEARS OF

WEST INDIES' CURTLY AMBROSE
TAKES A BREAK. 04/08/2000

OPPOSITE

ENGLAND'S NASSER HUSSAIN. 28/11/2000

ENGLAND'S DARREN GOUGH
REVIEWS HIS BOWLING TECHNIQUE.
10/12/2000

LANCASHIRE'S MICK SMETHURST
CELEBRATES. 08/08/2001

ENGLAND'S MARK BUTCHER IS ALL
SMILES AS HE LEAVES THE PITCH
WITH THE STUMPS AFTER LEADING
HIS SIDE TO VICTORY IN THE FOURTH
ASHES WITH A TOTAL OF 173 NOT
OUT. 20/08/2001

OPPOSITE

GLOUCESTERSHIRE'S JACK RUSSELL.
24/04/2003

ENGLAND CAPTAIN MICHAEL VAUGHAN (R) AND TEAM MATE ANDREW FLINTOFF
LEAVE THE FIELD AFTER DRAWING THE FIFTH TEST MATCH AGAINST SOUTH
AFRICA. 25/01/2005

SHANE WARNE, AUSTRALIA, BOWLING
AGAINST ENGLAND AT TRENT BRIDGE.
25/08/2005

ENGLAND'S PAUL COLLINGWOOD
AVOIDS A BOUNCER. 02/12/2005

ENGLAND'S MATTHEW HOGGARD (L)
AND ANDREW FLINTOFF (R).

05/06/2006

ENGLAND CAPTAIN ANDREW
FLINTOFF (C) LINES UP WITH HIS
TEAMMATES FOR A TEAM PICTURE.
06/11/2006

OPPOSITE

ENGLAND'S KEVIN PIETERSEN
CELEBRATES HIS CENTURY AGAINST
INDIA. 22/07/2007

ENGLAND'S MATTHEW HOGGARD.
25/11/2007

ENGLAND'S MONTY PANESAR
APPEALS. 26/11/2007

Chapter Two
PLACES

GREAT GROUNDS

Whether you are a spectator, a player or a visitor, one ground stands out above all others

There are other cricketing grounds worth a visit – the MCG in Melbourne has dignity, Adelaide has a beautiful view out over the cathedral and the city, Trinidad nestles in a lovely setting surrounded by the hills and Eden Gardens has the same life force as Calcutta itself – but Lord's beats them all.

THE LORD'S EXPERIENCE

Lord's nestles in St. Johns Wood, home to pop stars, as well as the rich and famous, and walking to the ground is an experience in itself. MCC members throng the streets, and seem to take over the route to the cricket ground.

They enter by the Grace Gates where uniformed officials check them in and make their way up the slight incline towards the back of the pavilion. On the left are the grand dining suite and the Harris Memorial garden. The Middlesex headquarters, the real

THE CROWDS PACK THE STANDS AT LORD'S. 24/06/1950

tennis court and the museum come next; on the right is found the back door into the pavilion. You must be one of the 18,000 members – or be part of an official tour – to enter those portals, once again guarded by the sort of doormen who guard the famous clubs in central London.

MEMBERS ONLY

One may have to wait many years to be a member of MCC but it is worth every penny of the annual fee since it brings privileges in Test match tickets and prestige. If the House of Commons is – as is commonly believed – the best club in town, then Lord's stands not far behind.

Up the stairs and straight ahead is the library, with tall chairs for those who wish to see out of the windows and newspapers for those who want to read. Turn right at the top of the stairs for the famous Long Room, where portraits of the great and good line

the walls, where more tall chairs are placed strategically so that the members have the finest view of the pitch and where, by convention if nothing else, quiet is maintained, even though the busy bar is not far away.

There is also a tiny lift that must be among the slowest anywhere in the world, but if crammed in there with a famous face the journey cannot last long enough.

Upstairs are the rooms essential for the game. Visitors' changing rooms on the left; England, Middlesex and

other home teams on the right. Committee rooms, players' dining rooms and physio rooms are at the end of long corridors and round unexpected corners. The whole tour may be an adventure.

Out into the fresh air again to walk past the Coronation Gardens with its informal picnics on match days on the left and the back of the Warner Stand - named for the famous England captain and man-about-Lord's Sir Pelham Warner – and here the observant may see the cars of the cricketers.

One Jaguar could always be identified by its number plate which set out Michael Colin Cowdrey's initials and his highest score. Cowdrey played for Kent all his life but he was so much a Lord's person that he brought his seven year old son Christopher to the ground, leaving young Chris with the strong impression that one day he might be able to call it his own.

Round beyond the tiny office that was once the headquarters of the International Cricket Conference (ICC) and the world game, the Nursery ground and the new media centre. This prize-winning structure is all the evidence anyone needs that the Lord's authorities are far from stuck in the 18th century, when they first established Lord's a mile away before buying the nursery and turning it into a cricket ground only four miles from the centre of London.

Pass the statues of batsman and bowler, pass the Nursery End nets and further backing for the futuristic thinking of those in charge comes when the Compton and Edrich Stands loom high above.

They are decorated with brightly coloured umbrellas – which led some to rechristen them The Umbrella Stands – but underneath are all the eating and drinking outlets a crowd of close to 30,000 spectators could need.

The Tavern used to stand at the next corner – another tradition gone forever – but soon we are beyond the area where sponsors as well as MCC and the England and Wales Cricket Board have their hospitality suites at the big matches, and back at the Grace Gates.

OTHER GREAT GROUNDS

Other great grounds include the riverside beauty of Worcester, the busy city venues at the Oval, also in London, Headingley in Leeds, Edgbaston in Birmingham, Old Trafford in Manchester and the developing site at Chester-le-Street, where the northern-most cricket ground in the world thrives although it is only a few years old.

GENERAL VIEW OF THE BRIT OVAL.
12/08/2007

TRENT BRIDGE, NOTTINGHAM.
12/08/2007

TRENT BRIDGE

Trent Bridge stands on the banks of the river as it flows through Nottingham. In one corner is found the old Trent Bridge Inn, still a hospitable place 200 years after it was run by William Clarke who wisely thought a cricket ground on the meadow at his back door might provide an added attraction. He later toured the country with a bunch of professionals happy to tackle 22 men of any other town or village and win a wager or two while they played.

HOSPITALITY

By and large, those who run cricket grounds are welcoming hosts whether they rule over Lord's, Northern Districts in New Zealand, that lovely little ground at Hobart in Tasmania or the village side at Little Puddlecome in the Marsh where the pavilion is an old garage and there is recent evidence of the cows who occupy the playing area every other day of the week.

From the traditional teas provided by the ladies' committee to the grand dinners put on, summer and winter, at Lord's, cricket has always been an eating man's game. Long may that tradition last!

THE OVAL DURING A MATCH.
04/06/1894

OPPOSITE

THE MARYLEBONE CRICKET CLUB
(MCC) LEAVE FOR SOUTH AFRICA
ON THE DECK OF THE SAXON. SEATED
ON THE WINDLASS (BOTTOM, THIRD
RIGHT) IS JOHNNY DOUGLAS
(CAPTAIN), TO HIS RIGHT IS SYDNEY
BARNES, AND FRANK WOOLLEY. 1913

A MATCH IN PROGRESS AT THE OVAL.
18/08/1934

OPPOSITE

A FACTORY AT ST JOHN'S WOOD, LONDON TRANSFORMING LUMPS OF WILLOW
INTO BATS. THE PICTURE SHOWS AN EMPLOYEE PLANING AND SHAPING THE
WILLOWS BEFORE PLACING THEM IN THE SPLICE. 27/03/1935

C.B. FRY AND FRIENDS WATCH A
MATCH FROM THE CLOCK TOWER
STAND AT LORD'S. 19/05/1945

OPPOSITE

LORD'S OFFICIALS HOLD BACK SPECTATORS WHO TRIED TO FORCE THE GRACE
GATES OPEN AFTER BEING LOCKED OUT DUE TO THE HUGE INTEREST IN THE
GAME BETWEEN ENGLAND AND AUSTRALIAN SERVICES. 14/07/1945

ROYAL AUSTRALIAN AIR FORCE AIRMEN WATCHING ENGLAND PLAY AUSTRALIAN SERVICES AT LORD'S. 14/07/1945

A LONG QUEUE FOR THE TEA BAR AT LORD'S. 14/07/1945

LUNCH TIME BY THE BOUNDARY
ROPE AT LORD'S. 07/08/1945

OPPOSITE

A SPECTATOR WITH A GOOD SUPPLY
OF ALCOHOL FOR THE AFTERNOON
SESSION AT LORD'S. 22/06/1946

SPECTATORS ENJOY A PINT WHILST WATCHING THE MATCH BETWEEN ENGLAND AND INDIA ON THE FIRST DAY OF PLAY AT LORD'S. 22/06/1946

OPPOSITE

NEWSPAPERS AND BOTTLES LITTER THE BOUNDARY AFTER THE DAY'S PLAY AT LORD'S. 27/06/1949

SPECTATORS AT THE ETON V HARROW
MATCH ENJOY A WALK ON THE
OUTFIELD DURING THE LUNCH
INTERVAL. 15/07/1946

OPPOSITE

THE PROSPECTIVE CRICKET COACHES
PRACTISE THEIR BATTING TECHNIQUE
EN MASSE, AT A COACHING SCHOOL
ORGANISED BY ESSEX CCC.
02/01/1950

SPECTATORS ENJOY A MATCH FROM
THE STANDS AT LORD'S. 19/05/1951

THE CROWD AT LORD'S. 19/05/1951

OPPOSITE

AN AERIAL VIEW OF THE OVAL AS PLAY
BETWEEN ENGLAND AND SOUTH
AFRICA TAKES PLACE. 16/08/1951

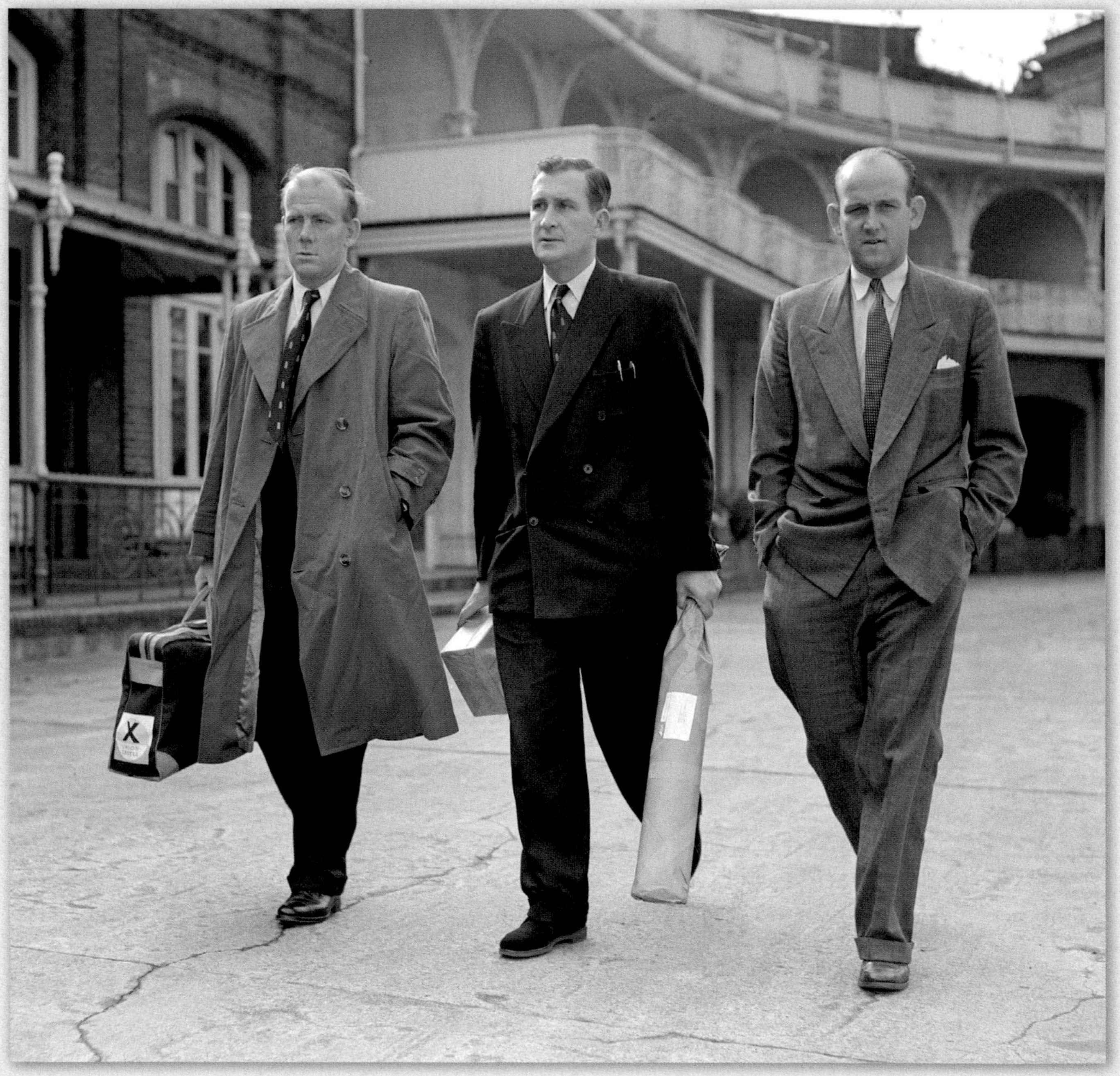

SPECTATORS ALLOWED A WALK ON
THE PITCH AT LUNCH DURING THE
ANNUAL CRICKET MATCH BETWEEN
ETON AND HARROW AT LORD'S.
01/07/1957

THE CROWD AT LORD'S. 18/08/1959

OPPOSITE

(L-R) ENGLAND'S JIM LAKER AND TONY LOCK HAVE THEIR TICKETS CHECKED
BEFORE BOARDING A TRAIN AT ST PANCRAS STATION ON THE FIRST LEG OF
THEIR JOURNEY TO AUSTRALIA. 14/09/1958

GROUNDSMEN AT THE ADELAIDE OVAL RETRIEVE THE BALL FROM THE ROOF OF ONE OF THE STANDS AFTER MCC CAPTAIN TED DEXTER HIT A SIX. 27/12/1962

VIEW OF LORD'S. 21/06/1963

OPPOSITE

FIVE DISAPPOINTED MEMBERS OF THE WEST INDIES PARTY SHELTER FROM THE
RAIN THAT PUT UP THE 'NO PLAY TODAY' NOTICES AT WORCESTER, WHERE THEY
SHOULD HAVE OPENED THEIR TOUR WITH THE CUSTOMARY MATCH AGAINST
THE HOME TEAM. 01/05/1963

OPPOSITE

WORLD HEAVYWEIGHT BOXING
CHAMPION MUHAMMAD ALI TAKES
IN THE VIEW FROM THE WEST INDIES'
DRESSING ROOM BALCONY AT
LORD'S. 16/05/1966

A WEST INDIES FAN DRESSED IN
CRICKET GEAR WAVES A FLAG IN
SUPPORT OF HIS TEAM, WHO WERE
PLAYING ENGLAND AT LORD'S.
20/06/1966

OPPOSITE

GARRY SOBERS, WEST INDIES
CAPTAIN, WAVES AS HE LEAVES
LONDON AIRPORT WITH OTHER
MEMBERS OF THE TEAM. ON THE
LEFT IS LANCE GIBBS AND RIGHT
MICHAEL CAREW. 14/09/1966

SOMERSET FANS IN FANCY DRESS
PARADE ROUND THE PITCH PRIOR TO
THE START OF A MATCH. 02/09/1967

THE CROWD UNDER UMBRELLAS WHILE PLAY IS SUSPENDED AT LORD'S. 20/06/1968

YOUNG SPECTATORS AMUSE
THEMSELVES WITH A GAME OF
IMPROMPTU CRICKET AS RAIN STOPS
PLAY AT LORD'S. 22/06/1968

AN ENGLAND FAN FINDS A NOVEL
WAY OF KEEPING DRY DURING A
RAINSTORM AT LORD'S. 22/06/1968

OPPOSITE

THE GROUNDSMAN AT LORD'S
SURROUNDS THE SQUARE WITH
A ROLL OF BARBED WIRE TO
PROTECT AGAINST PROTESTERS.
08/03/1970

PREVIOUS PAGE

CROWDS AT LORD'S. 22/06/1972

WEST INDIES SUPPORTERS AT THE
OVAL, WHERE THE WEST INDIES BEAT
ENGLAND BY 158 RUNS TO WIN THE
FIRST TEST. IT WAS THE WEST INDIES'
FIRST WIN IN 21 TESTS AND GAVE
THEM A 1-0 LEAD IN THE THREE
MATCH SERIES. 31/07/1973

OPPOSITE

A PLAYER LOOKS OUT OVER THE
PITCH FROM THE BALCONY OF
THE CHANGING ROOMS DURING
THE FIRST WOMEN'S MATCH TO BE
PLAYED AT LORD'S. 04/08/1976

CLIVE LLOYD (L), WEST INDIES
CAPTAIN CONDUCTS HIS SINGING
TEAM MEMBERS, DURING A
RECORDING SESSION AT THE
LANSDOWNE STUDIOS, HOLLAND
PARK. 29/08/1976

OPPOSITE
ENGLAND'S BOB WILLIS (L) AND IAN
BOTHAM (R) ENJOY A GAME OF 'TEST
MATCH' TABLE CRICKET. 25/10/1978

FIELDING PRACTICE AT LORD'S DURING THE FIRST WOMEN'S WEST INDIES CRICKET TEAM VISIT TO ENGLAND. 01/06/1979

(L-R) SURREY'S GRAHAM ROOPE, GEOFF HOWARTH AND ROBIN JACKMAN TEST CHELSEA FOOTBALL CLUB'S STAMFORD BRIDGE PITCH A WEEK BEFORE THEIR FLOODLIT MATCH AGAINST THE WEST INDIES. 06/08/1980

THE FLOODLIT CRICKET MATCH AT
CHELSEA FOOTBALL CLUB'S GROUND,
STAMFORD BRIDGE. 14/08/1980

OPPOSITE

BBC RADIO COMMENTATOR JOHN
ARLOTT PICTURED DURING THE FIRST
DAY OF HIS FINAL COMMENTARY.
28/08/1980

THE TWO CAPTAINS, OLD ENGLAND
XI'S FRED TRUEMAN (R) AND OLD
INTERNATIONAL XI'S GARRY SOBERS
(L), AWAIT THE OUTCOME OF THE
COIN TOSS. 17/09/1983

OPPOSITE

THE LONG ROOM AT LORD'S.
30/01/1984

(L-R) AUSTRALIA'S GREG RITCHIE, DAVID BOON, JEFF THOMSON AND CRAIG MCDERMOTT (BACK) HELP TO LOAD THE FIRST SHIPMENT OF BARRELS OF AUSTRALIAN LAGER CASTLEMAINE XXXX ONTO A HORSE-DRAWN DRAY FOR DELIVERY TO THE KING AND KEYS IN FLEET STREET. 15/05/1985

A LORD'S CRICKET FAN SITS WITH HIS
UMBRELLA AS PLAY IS ABANDONED.
22/06/1987

MCC MEMBERS QUEUE UP OUTSIDE THE GATES FOR THE START OF A TEST MATCH. 26/07/1990

VILLAGE CRICKET BEING PLAYED AT
CAR COLSTON, NOTTINGHAMSHIRE.
26/06/1993

FOLLOWING PAGE

TRENT BRIDGE ON THE FINAL DAY
OF THE FOURTH TEST BETWEEN
ENGLAND AND SOUTH AFRICA.
27/07/1998

OPPOSITE

THE NATWEST MEDIA CENTRE AT
LORD'S. 01/08/1999

WEST INDIES BOWLERS CURTLY
AMBROSE (L) AND COURTNEY WALSH
LEAVE THE FIELD AT THE END OF
ENGLAND'S SECOND INNINGS,
DURING THE FIFTH TEST AT THE
OVAL. 03/09/2000

A PAKISTAN CRICKET BOARD SELECT XI BAT AGAINST ENGLAND AS THE SUN SETS. 25/11/2000

DIGGERS REMOVE BOTH TURF AND FOUNDATIONS AT LORD'S. THE OUTFIELD WAS BEING TOTALLY REBUILT – DRAINAGE SYSTEMS AND ALL - FOR THE FIRST TIME IN THE HISTORY OF THE FAMOUS GROUND. 09/09/2002

CLIPSAL VISION

MITSUBISHI
MITSUBISHI MOTORS
Spirited Cars for Spirited People

ENGLAND CAPTAIN NASSER HUSSAIN
IS SHOWN ON A GIANT TELEVISION
SCREEN AT THE ADELAIDE OVAL,
AUSTRALIA. 23/11/2002

OPPOSITE
SIMON WILLIAMSON, ASSISTANT
HEAD GROUNDSMAN, SURVEYS WHAT
IS LEFT OF THE FAMOUS LIME TREE AT
THE ST LAWRENCE CRICKET GROUND,
THE HOME OF KENT COUNTY
CRICKET CLUB, AFTER IT WAS BLOWN
OVER IN HIGH WINDS. 10/01/2005

FANS WEAR RICHIE BENAUD MASKS

DURING ENGLAND V AUSTRALIA AT

TRENT BRIDGE. 25/08/2005

OPPOSITE

A CRICKET FAN AT LORD'S. 14/04/2006

PRIME MINISTER TONY BLAIR PLAYS CRICKET IN THE HALLWAY OF NO. 10 DOWNING STREET WITH MEMBERS OF EASTCOTE CRICKET CLUB IN HARROW BEFORE HOSTING A RECEPTION TO MARK THE OCCASION OF MR BLAIR BECOMING PATRON OF A SPORTS CLUB. 22/11/2006

WORCESTERSHIRE CRICKET GROUND NEW ROAD AFTER ITS FOURTH FLOOD
OF THE WINTER. THE RIVER SEVERN BURST ITS BANKS TO LEAVE MORE THAN
A FOOT OF WATER LYING ACROSS THE OUTFIELD AND SQUARE WITH ONLY SIX
WEEKS TO GO BEFORE THE OPENING COUNTY CHAMPIONSHIP CLASH WITH
DURHAM. 08/03/2007

SURREY BROWN CAPS V DURHAM DYNAMOS, GUILDFORD CRICKET CLUB. 29/07/2007

ENGLAND'S ANDREW STRAUSS IN ACTION AGAINST INDIA AS THE BRIT OVAL IS BATHED IN SUN. 12/08/2007

ENGLAND'S ANDREW FLINTOFF CLIMBS THE STEPS BACK TO THE PAVILION AFTER A TRAINING SESSION AT OLD TRAFFORD.

29/08/2007

ENGLAND'S MICHAEL VAUGHAN FIELDS AMONGST BIRDS DURING A TOUR MATCH AT COLOMBO CRICKET CLUB, COLOMBO, SRI LANKA. 21/11/2007

Chapter Three
MOMENTS

UPS AND DOWNS

Cricket is a game of drama and the unexpected

Test cricketers, and batsmen based in the southern counties in particular, often used to hate their annual trip to Headingley, particularly early in the season when it was cold enough to need two sweaters.

The pitch was always difficult and often prone to mood swings. One minute it was peaceful and friendly; two overs later it was a vicious strip on which the ball alternately lifted chest high or squatted so low that toes were in danger.

The pitch could be a nightmare for batsmen, heaven for medium fast bowlers and a joy for spectators.

The Ashes series of 1981 is a case in point. Botham, who had been dropped as Test captain at the end of the previous Test at Lord's, was transformed into a national hero in just three days.

The story of the game, with all its miraculous twists and turns, is well known to cricket lovers. Australia batted for 401 of which John Dyson, a stern opening batsman, made 102 and the captain Kim Hughes 89.

The Aussies were 1-0 ahead in the Test series and probably felt little pressure to move the game forward and although Botham, already one of the great England quick swing bowlers, took six for 95, that has been forgotten now alongside his amazing feats in the rest of the match.

HEADINGLEY. 01/08/1970

He also got 50 as England put together 174 in their first innings and had to follow on; the next highest score came from 34 extras. It seemed certain that England, led by Mike Brearley, recalled after Botham's dismissal, would be defeated comprehensively: especially when they lost seven wickets for 135 in their second innings.

With Dennis Lillee, even though he was on his last tour of England, at his rampaging best and Terry Alderman supporting him with his probing medium pace, there seemed to be no answer. The England players had checked out of their hotel and the result was such a foregone conclusion by lunch time on the fourth day that a bookmaker offered 500-1 on an England win.

Out in the middle Botham decided to chance his arm and, in a memorable stand with the fast bowler Graham Dilley, pulverised the Australian bowlers. The most memorable picture remaining in the mind's eye is of his audacious hooks against Lillee whose face tells its own story.

'I kept thinking 'he cannot have got away with it again,' he said years later. 'It seemed the ball just had to fall into the hands of deep square leg.' Instead the ball usually ended in the crowd as Botham raced to 149 not out, Dilley completed his first Test 50 and, with 29 from Chris Old on his home ground, England totalled 356 and set Australia to make 130 for what still appeared to be an easy victory.

When they did not lose their second wicket until 56 had been scored, when Dyson resumed the mood of his first innings and the pitch appeared to be playing true, forecasts of a 2-0 lead in the series were on everyone's lips.

Then the miracle Botham had begun was turned into a golden victory by Bob Willis who, eyes blazing and arms pumping in the manner which caused his action to be compared to a plane with a broken wing, tore through the last Australian batsmen and finished with eight for 43.

As the miracle unfolded stockbrokers ignored business and almost closed down the Stock Exchange, and Oxford Street came to a standstill.

Willis, in his TV interview on the balcony at the end of the game, criticised all the media who had said England were a beaten side.

By this time Botham, Willis and Brearley were the talk of the town, but in the next month England won the Ashes and the Australians returned home in defeat.

Eighteen months after that tussle at Headingley, on their next tour of Australia, England won the fourth Test – begun on Boxing Day as usual – by just three runs in front of a 40,000 crowd who had been allowed into the Melbourne Cricket Ground free so they could watch the last two Aussies Allan Border and Jeff Thomson go for victory.

Willis was captain by this time and the previous evening he had concentrated

EXHAUSTED ENGLAND HERO BOB WILLIS ON THE HEADINGLEY BALCONY AFTER TAKING EIGHT WICKETS IN AUSTRALIA'S SECOND INNINGS TO SEAL AN UNLIKELY ENGLAND VICTORY. 21/07/1981

on giving Border singles so that his bowlers could attack Thomson, the No.11 batsman.

The tactics were fair enough; unfortunately they did not work and for 90 minutes on the final morning it looked as if England had turned easy victory into embarrassing defeat.

Those who thought that way reckoned without the spirit of Botham who produced the ball that was required, which caught the edge of Thomson's bat and went at a comfortable height to Chris Tavare at slip.

Tavare, not surprisingly tense, could only parry the ball which ballooned into the air, straight to Geoff Miller who ran round behind him to take the catch that won a Test. It had finished in front of those sports mad Melbourne people who might only have seen one ball but whose passion for the game was duly rewarded with yet another dramatic finish.

Thomson's wicket was Botham's 100th against Australia, showing once again his sense of theatre. It underlined what Graham Gooch said to him when he took a wicket with his first Test delivery after a ban. 'Who writes your scripts for you?'
A quarter of a century down the way

Botham is now a star of the TV screen, and Miller is head of the England selection panel.

'That is an exciting job,' Miller said when he heard of his appointment. You can bet it is nothing like as exciting as the day he sealed a Test victory just when it seemed to have slipped from England's grasp.

ENGLAND'S ANDREW FLINTOFF CELEBRATES CLAIMING THE WICKET OF AUSTRALIA'S MATTHEW HAYDEN IN THE NPOWER FIFTH TEST AT THE BRIT OVAL. 11/09/2005

THE FIRST OFFICIAL AUSTRALIAN SIDE TO VISIT ENGLAND. 25/05/1878

AUSTRALIA'S BILL PONSFORD (L) LOOKS BACK TO SEE HIS SHOT FIELDED IN THE
SLIPS DURING A MATCH AGAINST OXFORD UNIVERSITY. 28/05/1930

OPPOSITE

YORKSHIRE'S PERCY HOLMES (L) AND
HERBERT SUTCLIFFE (R) CELEBRATE IN
FRONT OF THE SCOREBOARD AFTER
PUTTING ON A RECORD FIRST-CLASS
FIRST WICKET STAND OF 555, OF
WHICH HOLMES SCORED 224 AND
SUTCLIFFE 313, AT THE COUNTY
GROUND, LEYTON. 16/06/1932

KING GEORGE V IS INTRODUCED
TO THE ENGLAND AND AUSTRALIA
TEAMS BEFORE THE START OF THE
SECOND ASHES TEST. 22/06/1934

OPPOSITE
AT THE START OF THE SECOND ASHES TEST, ENGLAND CAPTAIN BOB WYATT (R) TOSSES THE COIN WITH HIS LEFT HAND, HIS RIGHT THUMB BEING IN A SPLINT, AS AUSTRALIA CAPTAIN BILL WOODFULL (L) CALLS. 22/06/1934

A FLYING BOMB LOOKED LIKE LANDING ON THE PRACTICE GROUND AT LORD'S, BUT FELL SOME 200 YARDS SHORT. THE PLAYERS AND UMPIRES LAY ON THE GROUND, AND SPECTATORS WERE TO BE SEEN IN CURIOUS POSTURES IN THE PAVILION AND AROUND THE GROUND. 29/07/1944

A YOUNG PHOTOGRAPHER (L) SNAPS
A PICTURE OF AUSTRALIA'S DON
BRADMAN AND ENGLAND'S NORMAN
YARDLEY AS THEY EMERGE FROM THE
PAVILION ONTO THE PITCH.
22/07/1948

OPPOSITE

AUSTRALIA'S DON BRADMAN MAKES HIS WAY BACK TO THE PAVILION THROUGH
CROWDS OF WELL-WISHERS AFTER HELPING HIS TEAM TO VICTORY WITH AN
UNBEATEN 173 ON THE FINAL DAY OF THE FOURTH ASHES TEST. AUSTRALIA SET
A NEW TEST RECORD (WHICH STOOD UNTIL 1975) BY SCORING 404 IN THEIR
SECOND INNINGS TO WIN THE GAME. 27/07/1948

AUSTRALIA'S DON BRADMAN (L)
CONGRATULATES TEAMMATE ARTHUR
MORRIS (R) ON REACHING HIS
CENTURY DURING THEIR SECOND
WICKET STAND OF 301 IN THE
FOURTH ASHES TEST. 27/07/1948

CAMBRIDGE UNIVERSITY'S HUBERT
DOGGART (L) AND JOHN DEWES (R)
STAND IN FRONT OF THE FENNER'S
SCOREBOARD, BY THEIR RESPECTIVE
FIRST INNINGS SCORES. BOTH MEN
REMAINED UNBEATEN THROUGHOUT
THE INNINGS, A SECOND WICKET
STAND OF 429. 09/05/1949

WICKETKEEPER GODFREY EVANS, IN
ACTION AGAINST THE WEST INDIES
AT TRENT BRIDGE. 03/05/1950

THE SCOREBOARD AT THE GABBA SHOWS THE INAUSPICIOUS BEGINNINGS
OF AUSTRALIA'S SECOND INNINGS AGAINST ENGLAND – THE FIRST THREE
BATSMEN, JACK MORONEY, ARTHUR MORRIS AND SAM LOXTON, ALL DISMISSED
FOR NO RUNS. 04/12/1950

ENGLAND'S FRANK TYSON
COLLAPSES AFTER BEING HIT ON
THE HEAD BY A BOUNCER FROM
AUSTRALIA'S RAY LINDWALL (NOT
IN PIC). HE WAS TAKEN TO HOSPITAL
FOR X-RAYS BUT LATER RESUMED HIS
INNINGS. 21/12/1954

OPPOSITE

YORKSHIRE'S FRED TRUEMAN (L)
HITS HIS SECOND SUCCESSIVE SIX
OF THE OVER AS MIDDLESEX
WICKETKEEPER LES COMPTON (R)
LOOKS ON. 18/07/1955

ENGLAND'S JIM LAKER IS APPLAUDED
OFF THE FIELD AFTER TAKING SIX
SECOND INNINGS WICKETS TO HELP
ENGLAND TO VICTORY IN THE THIRD
ASHES TEST. 17/07/1956

OPPOSITE
AUSTRALIA'S NEIL HARVEY (THIRD L) THROWS HIS BAT UP IN THE AIR AFTER
BEING DISMISSED BY ENGLAND'S JIM LAKER (THIRD R) FOR
THE SECOND TIME IN ONE DAY. 27/07/1956

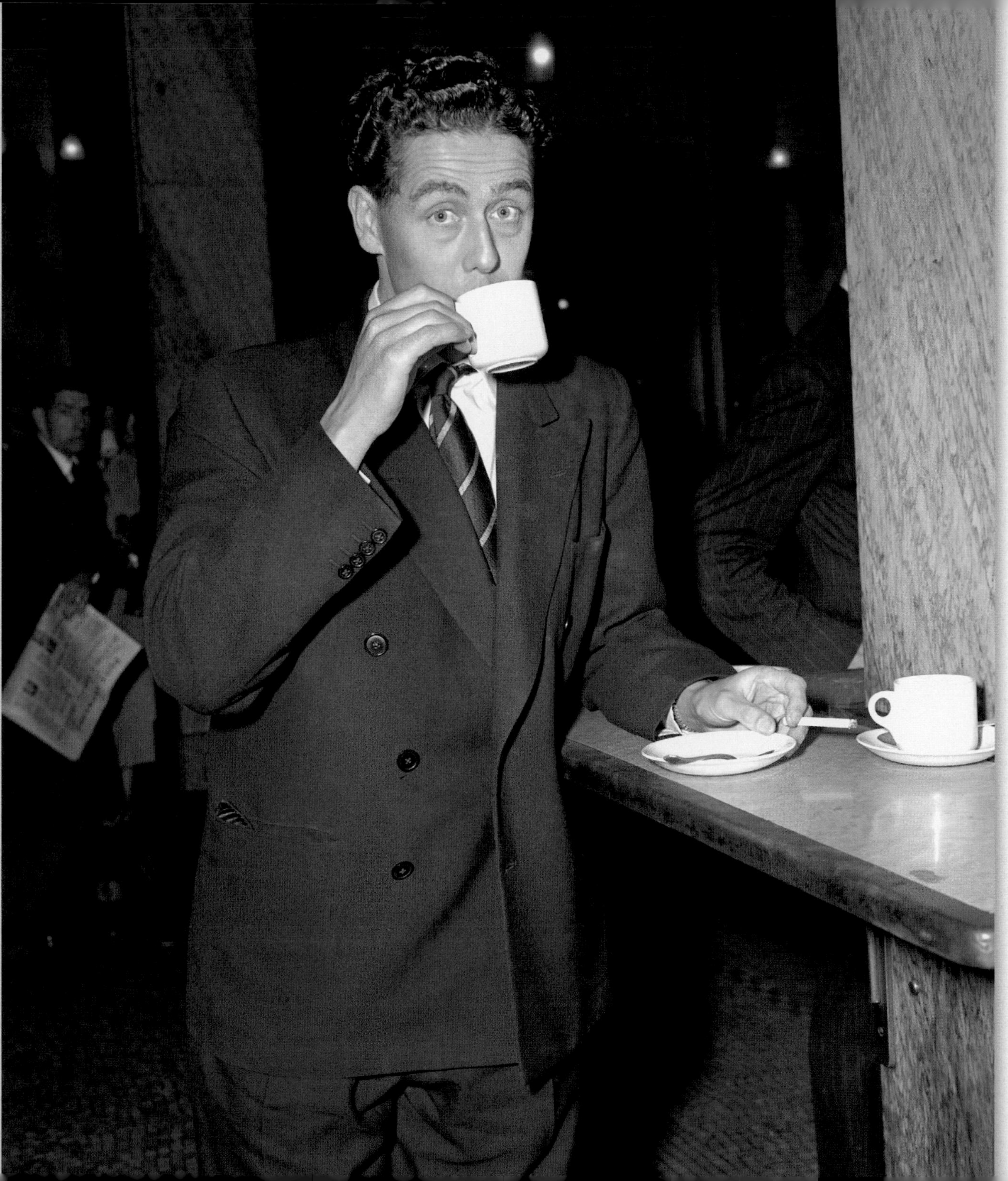

OPPOSITE

ENGLAND'S TREVOR BAILEY, WHO MISSED THE TRAIN CARRYING THE TOUR PARTY, RELAXES AT THE WATERLOO STATION BUFFET WHILE WAITING FOR THE NEXT TRAIN TO SOUTHAMPTON, FROM WHERE THE ENGLAND TEAM SET SAIL FOR SOUTH AFRICA. 04/10/1956

ENGLAND'S BRIAN STATHAM (FIFTH L) IS CONGRATULATED BY HIS TEAMMATES AFTER TAKING A HAT-TRICK AGAINST TRANSVAAL. 01/12/1956

WEST INDIES FANS CELEBRATE AS THE
FIRST THREE ENGLAND WICKETS FALL
CHEAPLY IN THE SECOND TEST AT
LORD'S. 20/06/1957

OPPOSITE

ENGLAND'S FRED TRUEMAN, WHO TOOK FIVE WICKETS FOR 58 RUNS, LEADS
THE TEAM INTO THE PAVILION AT THE CLOSE OF THE FIRST AUSTRALIAN
INNINGS IN THE THIRD ASHES TEST. 06/07/1961

ENGLAND'S TED DEXTER IS NEARLY
CAUGHT OUT AGAINST WEST INDIES,
BUT THE TWO FIELDERS ALLOW THE
BALL TO SLIP THROUGH THEIR
FINGERS. 27/07/1963

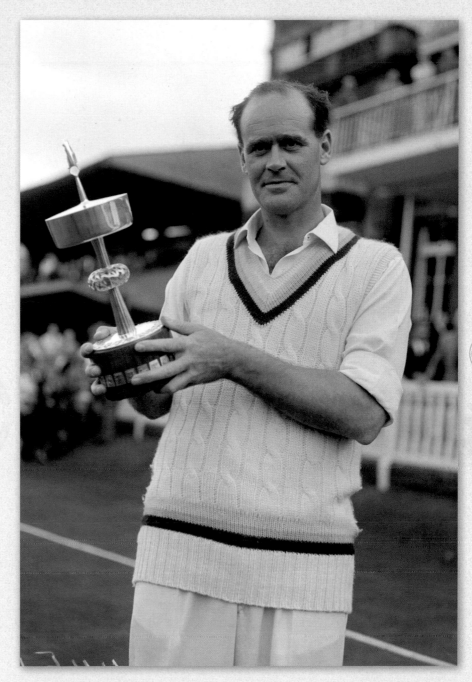

YORKSHIRE CAPTAIN BRIAN CLOSE
SHOWS OFF THE GILLETTE CUP AFTER
HIS TEAM'S VICTORY. 04/09/1965

YORKSHIRE'S GEOFF BOYCOTT
SHOWS OFF HIS SOUVENIR STUMP
AND MAN OF THE MATCH MEDAL,
WHICH HE EARNED BY RATTLING UP
146 RUNS AGAINST SURREY IN THE
GILLETTE CUP FINAL. 04/09/1965

OPPOSITE

WORLD HEAVYWEIGHT BOXING
CHAMPION MUHAMMAD ALI
PRACTISES HIS BATTING TECHNIQUE
IN THE WEST INDIES DRESSING
ROOM AT LORD'S, TO THE
AMUSEMENT OF THE PLAYERS.
16/05/1966

OPPOSITE

WEST INDIES FANS CONGRATULATE
DAVID HOLFORD ON REACHING HIS
CENTURY AGAINST ENGLAND.
21/06/1966

WARWICKSHIRE CAPTAIN, AND MAN
OF THE MATCH, ALAN SMITH HOLDS
THE GILLETTE CUP ALOFT AS HE IS
CHAIRED BY HIS TRIUMPHANT
TEAMMATES. 07/09/1968

REST OF THE WORLD'S GARRY SOBERS IS SURROUNDED BY YOUNG AUTOGRAPH HUNTING FANS AFTER TAKING SIX WICKETS FOR 21 RUNS IN ENGLAND XI'S FIRST INNINGS. 17/06/1970

OPPOSITE

LEICESTERSHIRE FANS SWARM ONTO THE PITCH TO CELEBRATE AFTER BEATING YORKSHIRE IN THE BENSON & HEDGES CUP FINAL. 22/07/1972

OPPOSITE

A STREAKER HURDLES STUMPS
AT LORD'S DURING A TEST MATCH.
04/08/1975

WEST INDIES FANS CELEBRATE
BATSMAN VIV RICHARDS REACHING
HIS DOUBLE CENTURY AGAINST
ENGLAND. 04/06/1976

A HIGH MOMENT FOR VIV RICHARDS AS HE ATTAINS HIS HALF CENTURY AGAINST ENGLAND AND AN EXCITED FAN RUNS ONTO THE HEADINGLEY PITCH TO HOIST HIM SKYWARDS. *22/07/1976*

OPPOSITE

THE WEST INDIES FIELDERS JUMP WITH DELIGHT AS ENGLAND'S BOB WOOLMER IS OUT FOR LBW, BOWLED BY MIKE HOLDING FOR EIGHT. *14/08/1976*

MIDDLESEX CAPTAIN MIKE BREARLEY
(C) SWIGS FROM A BOTTLE OF
CHAMPAGNE AS HE CELEBRATES
WITH HIS TEAMMATES AFTER THEIR
FIVE WICKET WIN OVER SURREY
CLINCHED THE COUNTY
CHAMPIONSHIP TITLE. 03/09/1976

OPPOSITE

GLOUCESTERSHIRE FANS CELEBRATE
AFTER BEATING KENT IN THE BENSON
& HEDGES CUP FINAL. 16/07/1977

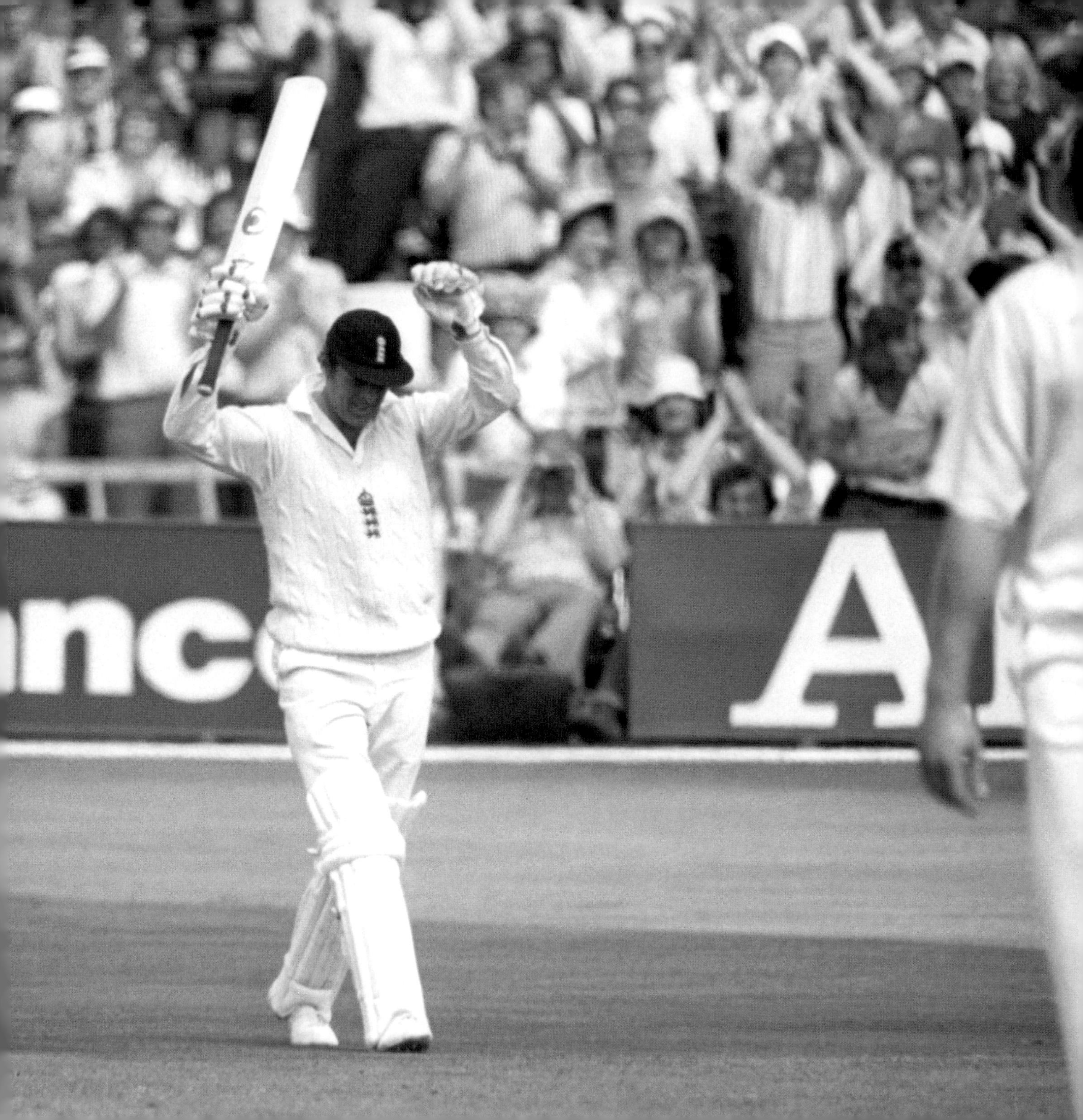

(L-R) ENGLAND'S DEREK RANDALL AND GEOFF BOYCOTT, WHO HAD RUN OUT
RANDALL IN THE FIRST INNINGS, WALK OFF THE PITCH TOGETHER AFTER
WRAPPING UP VICTORY IN ENGLAND'S SECOND INNINGS IN THE THIRD ASHES
TEST. 02/08/1977

OPPOSITE

ENGLAND'S GEOFF BOYCOTT
CELEBRATES REACHING HIS CENTURY
IN HIS FIRST TEST MATCH FOR THREE
YEARS. 30/07/1977

ENGLAND'S GEOFF BOYCOTT ON THE BALCONY AT TRENT
BRIDGE CELEBRATING VICTORY AGAINST AUSTRALIA IN
THE THIRD ASHES TEST. 02/08/1977

OPPOSITE

ENGLAND'S GEOFF BOYCOTT IS
MOBBED BY FANS AFTER
COMPLETING HIS 100TH TEST
CENTURY. 11/08/1977

MCC'S IAN BOTHAM (L) IS PRESENTED WITH THE BALL WITH WHICH HE TOOK

A HAT-TRICK DURING THE FIRST DAY'S PLAY AGAINST MIDDLESEX. 21/04/1978

ENGLAND'S IAN BOTHAM CELEBRATES AFTER TAKING EIGHT WICKETS FOR 34
RUNS IN PAKISTAN'S SECOND INNINGS TO HELP ENGLAND TO AN INNINGS
VICTORY. 19/06/1978

(L-R) SUSSEX CAPTAIN ARNOLD LONG HOLDS UP THE GILLETTE CUP, WATCHED
BY MAN OF THE MATCH PAUL PARKER AND A HUGE CROWD OF JUBILANT
SUSSEX FANS. 02/09/1978

OPPOSITE

JOEL GARNER, WEST INDIES, HOLDS
ALOFT THE PRUDENTIAL WORLD CUP
TROPHY. 24/06/1979

SOMERSET CAPTAIN BRIAN ROSE (R)
AND MAN OF THE MATCH VIV
RICHARDS (L) HOLD THE GILLETTE
CUP ALOFT. 08/09/1979

OPPOSITE
AUSTRALIA'S GRAHAM YALLOP IS CAUGHT OUT BY MAN OF THE MATCH IAN
BOTHAM (THIRD R) DURING THE FOURTH CORNHILL TEST MATCH AT
EDGBASTON. 02/08/1981

ENGLAND'S GEOFF BOYCOTT RACES
BACK TO THE EDGBASTON PAVILION
AS JUBILANT ENGLAND FANS POUR
ONTO THE PITCH TO CELEBRATE
VICTORY OVER AUSTRALIA. 02/08/1981

ENGLAND'S GEOFF BOYCOTT (R)
SHAKES HANDS WITH A FAN IN A
GORILLA SUIT WHO DECIDED TO GO
FOR A STROLL ON THE PITCH DURING
THE LAST DAY OF THE FIFTH TEST
AGAINST AUSTRALIA. 17/08/1981

JUBILANT DERBYSHIRE PLAYERS JOIN
CAPTAIN BARRY WOOD (ARM RAISED)
IN SHOWING THE NATWEST BANK
TROPHY TO THEIR SUPPORTERS AT
LORD'S. 05/09/1981

MAN OF THE MATCH, INDIA'S KAPIL DEV, CELEBRATES ON THE PAVILION BALCONY AT LORD'S DESPITE HIS TEAM'S DEFEAT AGAINST ENGLAND. 15/06/1982

SOMERSET CAPTAIN BRIAN ROSE HOLDS THE BENSON & HEDGES CUP ALOFT
FOR SUPPORTERS TO SEE AT LORD'S AFTER THEIR NINE WICKET VICTORY OVER
NOTTINGHAMSHIRE IN THE FINAL OF THE COMPETITION. 24/07/1982

SOMERSET CAPTAIN IAN BOTHAM
HOLDS THE NATWEST TROPHY ALOFT
AFTER HIS TEAM'S VICTORY.
03/09/1983

WEST INDIES' VIV RICHARDS GATHERS
HIS THOUGHTS DURING HIS RECORD-
BREAKING INNINGS OF 189 NOT OUT
AGAINST ENGLAND. 31/05/1984

FIZZY SHAMPOO FOR ENGLAND'S
VICTORIOUS CAPTAIN, DAVID GOWER,
WHO IS HOLDING A REPLICA OF THE
ASHES TROPHY. 02/09/1985

THE INDIAN CRICKET TEAM
CELEBRATE VICTORY OVER ENGLAND
AFTER WINNING THE SECOND TEST
AND THE SERIES, IN THE PAVILION
AT HEADINGLEY. 23/06/1986

ENGLAND'S DAVID GOWER (L) IS
CLEAN BOWLED BY PAKISTAN'S
IMRAN KHAN (R) FOR 10. 02/07/1987

NOTTINGHAMSHIRE'S RICHARD
HADLEE CELEBRATES AFTER HITTING
THE WINNING RUNS AGAINST
NORTHAMPTONSHIRE IN THE
NATWEST TROPHY FINAL. 07/09/1987

NOTTINGHAMSHIRE'S CLIVE RICE (L) AND RICHARD HADLEE CELEBRATE AT
TRENT BRIDGE AFTER WINNING THE COUNTY CHAMPIONSHIP. 14/09/1987

WEST INDIES CAPTAIN VIV RICHARDS AND TEAMMATE GUS LOGIE, MAN OF THE MATCH, CELEBRATE WINNING THE SECOND TEST AGAINST ENGLAND. 21/06/1988

NEW ZEALAND CAPTAIN RICHARD HADLEE (R) CELEBRATES AS ENGLAND
CAPTAIN GRAHAM GOOCH (L) IS DISMISSED LBW FIRST BALL. 09/06/1990

BRIAN LARA, WEST INDIES, WALKS
THROUGH A BRIDGE OF BATS AFTER
HIS RECORD-BREAKING INNINGS
AGAINST ENGLAND. 18/04/1994

ENGLAND'S IAN SALISBURY IS
TRAPPED LBW BY SRI LANKA'S
MUTHIAH MURALITHARAN.
31/08/1998

ENGLAND'S ANDREW FLINTOFF CELEBRATES AFTER DISMISSING AUSTRALIA'S
SHANE WARNE IN THE NPOWER THIRD TEST AT OLD TRAFFORD. 15/08/2005

AN ENGLAND PLAYER HOLDS THE ASHES URN ALOFT. 12/09/2005

ENGLAND'S SARAH TAYLOR
CELEBRATES THE WICKET OF INDIA'S
HEMLATA KALA. 14/08/2006

AUSTRALIA'S SHANE WARNE
SUCCESSFULLY APPEALS FOR THE
WICKET OF ENGLAND'S IAN BELL
DURING THE FOURTH DAY OF THE
FIRST TEST MATCH AT THE GABBA,
BRISBANE, AUSTRALIA. 26/11/2006

ENGLAND'S JAMES ANDERSON
LEAVES THE FIELD AT THE END OF
THE FIRST TEST MATCH AGAINST
AUSTRALIA AT THE GABBA, BRISBANE,
AUSTRALIA. 27/11/2006

OPPOSITE

ENGLAND'S KEVIN PIETERSEN
CELEBRATES AFTER REACHING HIS
CENTURY DURING THE FIRST DAY OF
THE SECOND NPOWER TEST MATCH
AT HEADINGLEY. 25/05/2007

The Publishers gratefully acknowledge PA Photos, from whose extensive archive – including The Press Association, Barratts and Sport & General collections – the photographs in this book have been selected.

Personal copies of the photographs in this book, and many others, may be ordered online at www.prints.paphotos.com

AMMONITE PRESS

For more information, please contact:

AMMONITE PRESS

AE Publications Ltd. 166 High Street, Lewes, East Sussex, BN7 1XU, United Kingdom

Tel: 01273 488005 Fax: 01273 402866

www.ae-publications.com